HOCKEY

Contents

Published by Heinemann Library
an imprint of Heinemann Publishers (Oxford) Ltd
Halley Court, Jordan Hill, Oxford OX2 8EJ

OXFORD LONDON EDINBURGH MADRID ATHENS BOLOGNA
PARIS MELBOURNE SYDNEY AUCKLAND SINGAPORE TOKYO
IBADAN NAIROBI HARARE GABORONE PORTSMOUTH NH (USA)

© 1994 Heinemann Library

98 97 96 95 94
10 9 8 7 6 5 4 3 2 1

British Library Cataloguing in Publication Data
Marshall, David
  Hockey. – (Successful Sports Series)
  I. Title II. Series
  796.355

ISBN 0 431 07432 1

Designed by Ron Kamen, Green Door Design Ltd, Basingstoke, England
Illustrated by Barry Atkinson
Printed in China

Acknowledgements
The Publishers would like to thank the following for permission to
reproduce photographs:

Action-plus: pp.26, 28, 29; Allsport: imprint, pp. 10, 12, 17 (bottom), 19,
23, 27; Colorsport: pp. 1, 3, 4, 5, 7, 8, 9, 13, 15, 17 (top); Meg Sullivan
and Andrew Waters: pp. 11, 14, 20, 21, 25.

Cover photograph © Colorsport

Thanks to Mike Hamilton of the Hockey Association for his comments.

The Publishers have made every effort to trace copyright holders.
However, if any material has been incorrectly acknowledged, we would
be pleased to correct this at the earliest opportunity.

Introduction

It is impossible to say when hockey began. There are Ancient Egyptian and Greek wall paintings from as far back as the 3rd century BC which show a game very like hockey. The Romans played a game with curved sticks and a leather ball, too. Although the modern sport is based on British games like bandy and shinty which are also played with curved sticks, the name hockey is thought to come from the French word *hoquet*, which means 'a hooked stick'.

The Hockey Association was founded in London in 1886. The British army helped to spread the game to India and the Far East. International competitions began in 1895. In India the game became popular so quickly that by 1928 it was the national game.

Women began playing organized hockey games in 1895. Even though the International Federation of Women's Hockey Associations was founded in 1927, women did not play serious international matches until the 1970s. The first Women's World Cup was held in 1974.

Egypt and Great Britain battle it out at the Barcelona Olympics in 1992.

Today the game is played all over the world and there are separate cups and leagues for men, women, mixed and junior hockey teams.

The pitch, ball and stick

Hockey is played between two teams of eleven players. The basic idea is to get possession of the ball and, by hitting it with the hockey stick, put it into the opposition's goal. Hockey is supposed to be a non-contact sport, which means players are not supposed to touch each other during the game.

The standard hockey pitch is a rectangle 91.5 m long (100 yds) and 54.9 m wide (60 yds). There is a centre line and two dotted lines 22.9 m (25 yds) from each end line. There is a semicircle of 14.6 m (16 yds) radius around each goal which is also known as the 'D' or **striking circle**. The penalty spot is just 6.4 m (7 yds) from the goal. The goal is small – only 3.6 m (12 ft) wide and 2.1 m (7 ft) high.

The game is sometimes called 'field hockey' because it always used to be played on grass pitches. Many clubs are playing on artificial pitches now. These allow play whatever the weather, and the ball should bounce evenly and travel in a straight line.

54.9 m (60 yds)
GOAL LINE
STRIKING CIRCLE
22.9 m (25 yds) LINE
CENTRE LINE
91.5 m (100 yds)
UMPIRE
FORWARDS
MIDFIELD PLAYERS
DEFENDER
SWEEPER
PENALTY SPOT
GOALKEEPER
4.6 m (5 yds) LINE
14.6 m (16 yds)

The pitch.

The ball is white and must weigh between 156 and 163 grams (5.5 to 5.75 ounces). It can be hollow or solid. It should be between 22.4 and 23.5 cm (about 9 in) round the circumference. Balls used to be made of leather, but are now made of plastic. The surface can be dimpled or smooth.

The stick is usually made of wood. The handle used to be made of cane, with a curved head of ash or mulberry. Recently, fibreglass and plastics have been used to make sticks. The head cannot be longer than 10 cm (4 in) and no part of the stick can be more than 5 cm (2 in) wide. One side of the head is flat and the other is round. Only the flat side can be used to hit the ball. Sticks can vary in weight from 340 grams (12 ounces) to 793 grams (28 ounces). Old-fashioned sticks used to be much longer. Today the game is faster and so the size and shape of the stick has been changed.

Pointers

You should have your own stick, but do not buy one until you have played the game for a while and know the weight of stick that suits you best. You should never use a stick that is too heavy because stick control is an important part of the game. No one can control a stick that is too heavy or too long for them.

The kit

The hockey kit is very simple and traditional. Men wear shirts and shorts, and women wear shirts and skirts. Players in a team all wear the same colour shirts, except for the goalkeeper who must wear a different colour. The shirts are numbered on the back to identify the players, but not their positions. Shorts, skirts and socks are also the same for all members of a team.

All players wear shin and ankle pads because the ball is hard. It is a good idea to protect your hands and fingers with protective gloves, and to use a gum shield. The boots worn will depend on the kind of pitch. On a grass pitch, football-style studded boots are worn. Special lightweight boots with moulded soles and many small pimples are worn on synthetic pitches.

Goalkeepers are the only players allowed to touch the ball with their feet. They often kick the ball out to their team mates, and so have to wear hard **kickers** over their boots for protection. Some international players can hit the ball at over 160 kph (100 mph) and so all goalkeepers wear pads on their legs, and padding to protect the rest of their bodies. They must always wear a helmet with a face mask. Goalkeepers wear gloves, too. For a right-handed goalkeeper the left glove is hard, padded and rigid, and is used for stopping the ball. The right glove is softer so that it can grip the stick. The padding on the gloves goes down over the wrists to protect the forearms. Despite all this padding and extra weight the goalkeeper has to be able to move quickly in any direction.

The goalkeeper wears a lot of protective clothing.

The line-up and tactic.

The eleven players on the field are usually arranged in a 5–3–2–1 formation. This means there are five forwards (attackers), three players in midfield, two backs (defenders) and the goalkeeper. The main reason for this line-up is that it allows the midfield to play easily, both in defence and attack. This is the old-fashioned football line-up and is used by clubs and schools.

KEY

GK   Goalkeeper
RB   Right Back
LB   Left Back
RH   Right Half
LH   Left Half
CB   Centre Back
CH   Centre Half
RW   Right Wing
LW   Left Wing
IR   Inside Right
IL   Inside Left
CF   Centre Forward

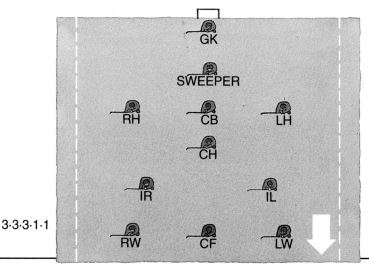

5·3·2·1

An alternative is the 3–3–3–1–1 formation. This means there are three forwards, three in midfield and three at the back. Right at the back there is a free defender who, as in football, is called a **sweeper**. It is their job to sweep up any attack that gets past the defence.

The two different line-ups.

3·3·3·1·1

For the players to be successful, whatever line-up they choose, they should plan in advance the tactics they are going to use in the game. If they are playing a team that is well known for having a good defence, they must be prepared to be patient and build up their attacks slowly and carefully. It is no use going out and just running at their opponents. Working out in advance what each player in the team is going to do at penalty corners and corners is also important, both in attack and defence. Nothing looks worse, or gives opponents more confidence, than a team which appears uncertain about what they are doing.

Sean Kerly is a centre-forward who often broke through the best defences!

The grip and dribbling

The first picture shows the basic grip of a hockey stick. For a right-handed player the left hand should be near the top of the stick and be used for twisting and turning the stick. The right hand is about 30 cm (12 in) further down the handle and holds the stick more firmly to give stability and control. The grip will change for the different types of shots played.

Mandy Nicholls demonstrates the basic grip of a hockey stick.

Dribbling, or running with the ball in front of you while keeping it under control, is another basic hockey skill. A player can only control the ball with the flat side of the stick. So when dribbling the ball, the stick must be turned over.

Dribbling is useful for getting out of trouble in defence when a **pass** would give the ball away, and for getting into a shooting position. However, it is difficult, and it can lead to loss of the ball.

Dribbling, shown in this Olympic game between India and Australia.

Players should always pass the ball when they can. If a player runs up and down the pitch with the ball, it is only going at his or her speed. If the ball is passed from player to player it will go forward much faster, and no single player will get as tired. It is called 'making the ball do the work'.

In an **Indian dribble**, so called because the Indian players became the world's greatest experts at it, the ball is tapped or dragged from side to side as the player runs forward, as shown in the picture. To do this the player must be able to turn the stick in his or her hands while running forward with the ball. If the stick is not turned then the ball will be hit with the wrong side, and a free hit will be given away. This kind of dribble takes a lot of practice.

Pointers

One thing to ask yourself before setting off on a dribble down the field is 'Am I doing this because I can help my team and get in a good position, or because I am being selfish and enjoy running with the ball?' Remember, it is always better to pass if you can.

Passing the ball

Hockey is a team game and so the most important skill of all is how to pass well to other players in the team. There are many different types of pass that can be used to get the ball from one player to another.

The **push** is the most important pass in the game. The ball will travel along the ground from a push. The left hand stays at the top of the stick but the right hand goes further down. You should point your left foot and shoulder towards the player you are passing to. First, the ball should be almost behind you, level with your right foot. From this position, push the ball along the ground, keeping the stick down and in contact with the ball for as long as possible. The stick should point towards the player receiving the ball at the end of the pass, as shown in the picture.

The **slap pass** is very similar to the push except as the stick is moved down to the ball the player moves his or her weight from the back foot to the front. The ball should be further forward than in the push. The right hand is pushed forward as the ball is hit in a sweeping movement. This sends the ball forward much faster than with a push.

A slap.

The **flick** is really the same as the push, except that the ball should be well in front of the player when it is flicked. The flat face of the stick should be underneath the ball, which lifts it upward and forward. Great care should be taken with this shot as the ball will be sent into the air. If it is played carelessly then a free hit could be given against you.

The most difficult pass is the **reverse-stick pass**. This is only played to make short passes and can be used only to send the ball from left to right. The ball should be close to the right foot as the ball is played with the toe of the stick.

The hit is the most powerful shot and pass in hockey and is used for long passes and for shots at the goal. The grip for this is different from the others – both hands should be together at the top of the stick, gripping it firmly. The hitter should have his or her weight on the back foot as the stick is swung back. On the downswing the weight is moved on to the front foot to give as much power as possible to the hit. The picture shows how the stick should follow through in front, in the direction the ball is going.

A hit.

Receiving the ball and beating defenders

To be a good hockey player you need to know how to take or receive the ball as well as pass it. If the ball comes along the ground, you should hold the stick in the usual way, and keep your weight well over the ball by bending the knees and leaning forward from the waist.

When the ball arrives at the stick, pull back the lower, right hand so the stick is angled down. The right hand should be relaxed as the ball arrives so the ball does not rebound. Study the photograph (left) to see how this is done.

If the ball comes at you through the air, the same skills are involved. You should keep the right hand relaxed so that the ball drops down and does not bounce away. The stick should be angled down so that the ball drops to your feet. The ball should never be played unless it is at shoulder level or below. Sometimes the reverse of the stick has to be used. As shown in the photograph (right), the toe of the stick must be pointing down.

Receiving the ball on the ground.

In a full match hockey players run several kilometres, so they have to be fit. Players are constantly stopping, starting and changing direction. It is worth just carrying a stick and practising this without a ball. As well as sprinting with the ball it is important to learn how to keep your eye on the play and run into open spaces when you have not got the ball. Your team mates will find it hard to pass to you if you are not in an open space. You must try and get well away from the opposition's defenders.

Getting past a defender when you have the ball is a difficult skill. It is always better to pass to a team mate if you can. The only way to get past a defender is to fool your opponent into thinking you are going one way, and then go the other. You can do this by leaning one way and then at the last minute changing direction. This is a skill that must be practised. Two players can help each other. One player must stand and try not to get in the way. The other should run at him or her and dodge, first one way and then the other. It is important to practise going round both sides of the defender.

Receiving the ball in the air.

Defending, marking and tackling

When you lose the ball you must try to get it back as soon as possible, and make sure the other team does not score. The usual way to defend against the players in the other team is known as marking. This means keeping one player in particular in your sights – if you want to have an easy game you have to hope it is not the opposition's star player! You keep as close as you can to the player you are marking so that if he or she gets a pass you can either intercept it, or make a quick tackle before your opponent has gained control of the ball. You should try to get between your goal and the player you are marking. This is called **getting goal side**.

If you are making a tackle, be bold. A half-hearted tackle is likely to fail or give away a free hit. In all tackles you must keep watching the ball. Do not be fooled by what your opponent is doing. You should keep the head of your stick near the ground and as close to the ball as possible. This will make your opponent wonder what to do with the ball, or perhaps force him or her to make a mistake.

The **jab tackle** is where you get as close to the ball as you can and, holding the stick in the left hand, jab the ball away from your opponent.

The block tackle.

You should not stretch too far to make this tackle, because if you miss you must be ready to go on and quickly make another attempt.

The **open-side**, or block tackle is the most common in the game. It is simply where an opponent tries to get past you on your right. You get alongside, or in front, and put your stick on the ball as it arrives. You cannot just stand in the way as this would be obstruction and would give away a free hit.

The **reverse-stick** tackle is much more difficult and is used when a player tries to go past you on the left. The idea is to allow the attacker to get level with you, and with the stick just in your left hand you hook the stick over the ball. You can then drag the ball away from the attacker as he or she goes by. This is a difficult tackle because you must not make contact with your opponent's body or stick.

A last ditch, desperate dive tackle.

Shooting and goalkeeping

The most difficult and dangerous position on the field is that of goalkeeper. The goalkeeper has to prevent goals being scored. Players can only shoot at goal when they are in the striking circle. If the ball goes into the goal after it is hit from outside the circle the goal does not count. Although it is important to be able to shoot using the slap and hit strokes, most goals are scored because players are alert and ready for any rebounds and deflections that happen in the circle.

There are a lot of rebounds in hockey because the goalkeeper cannot catch or hold the ball. The goalkeeper is not allowed to hit the ball with a hand or the body. They can only stop the ball. They must then kick the ball away.

Pointers

It is important for a goalkeeper to be able to stop and kick the ball away in one movement. Usually there is not enough time to stop and then kick the ball.

The goalkeeper's basic stance is shown in the picture on page 5. From this position they must be able to move quickly in any direction. If the goalkeeper cannot stop the ball with their body because the ball is too far away, then they must use their hand. The right-hand glove is softer to allow the goalkeeper to hold their stick.

The left-hand glove is heavily padded and is used to make saves. If the ball is still too far away to reach, the goalkeeper can use their stick to make a save. The stick should be used only as a last resort.

If you are a goalkeeper and have to dive to stop the ball, try not to go down on the ground – it is difficult to get up again in all that protective clothing!

Indoor hockey

A variation on the traditional game of hockey is **indoor hockey**. This game began in Germany and Holland so that players could practise when the weather was too bad to play outside. Indoor hockey is now a game in its own right. A maximum of six players per team can be on the pitch at any time. An outdoor squad can divide into two teams and play indoor hockey for practice.

The ball for indoor hockey is the same as for the outdoor game, except it is smooth on the outside and weighs 156–163 grams (5.5–5.75 ounces). The ball is pushed and cannot be hit. The sticks used are much lighter and have a shorter head. When a player pushes the ball the stick must travel along the ground and not be lifted. When **clearing** the ball, the goalkeeper must make sure the ball is kept on the ground.

The indoor pitch.

NO BOARD

SHOOTING CIRCLE

SIDE BOARD

36–44 m (39–48 yds)

CENTRE LINE

9 m (10 yds)

GOAL

GOAL LINE 18–22 m (20–24 yds)

The indoor pitch is smaller – between 36 and 44 m (39 and 48 yds) long, and between 18 and 22 m (20 and 24 yds) wide. The goals are 3 m (10 ft) across and 2 m (7 ft) high. There should be side boards down both sides of the pitch. These are just 10 cm (4 in) high.

Because the pitch is small the game is fast. Players have to both attack and defend. As there is little space it is hard to get away from, or round, other players. This means players have to be very skilful in using their sticks to dribble and pass. The need to dribble and pass well helps everyone improve their skills, ready for the open spaces of the outdoor game.

The constant movement in indoor hockey means games cannot last long. The length of games varies between ten and twenty minutes in each of two halves. Substitutes are allowed at any time during the game, but a team must never have less than four or more than six players on the pitch at any time.

An action-packed indoor hockey game.

Starting the game, free hits and push-ins

The traditional, outdoor game is played over two 35 minute periods, with a half-time of around 10 minutes in between. At the end of each half extra time is played to make up for any injury time. The team that has scored the most goals by the end of the game is the winner. For a goal to be scored, the whole of the ball must be over the goal line, between the posts, and under the bar.

The game used to be started with the traditional **bully-off**. This is still used in the game but not at the start. The two captains toss a coin to decide who should have the ball at the start, or which end to attack in the first half. At the start of play, whichever team has the ball must play a **pass-back** to one of its own players. All players must be in their own half of the field to begin. The players in the team without the ball must all be at least 4.6 m (5 yds) away from the ball when the ball is first hit or pushed. A pass-back like this also restarts the game after a goal has been scored.

A push in.

When the ball goes out over the side lines a player from the team that did not hit the ball out has to push or hit the ball back into play from the spot where it went out. All the opposing players must be at least 4.6 m (5 yds) away.

The most common foul in hockey is **feet**. When the ball touches a player's foot, a free hit is awarded to the opposing team. Free hits are always awarded to the side who are fouled, and are taken from where the offence was committed. The ball must not be moving when the free hit is taken, and must not be lifted into the air. The player taking the free hit cannot touch the ball again until another player has hit it.

A free hit.

Corners, fouls and penalties

When the ball goes off the pitch over the goal line, there are three ways for the game to restart if a goal has not been scored. If an attacker knocks the ball over the line or if a defender accidentally knocks the ball out from over 22.9 m (25 yds) away, then the defending team restarts the game from a point 14.6 m (16 yds) from where it went out.

If a defender accidentally knocks the ball out over the goal line from less than 22.9 m (25 yds) away, then the attackers are given a **corner** from within 2.7 m (3 yds) of the corner. This used to be called a 'long corner'. Attackers can stand anywhere on the pitch. Defenders can stand anywhere except within 4.6 m (5 yds) of the ball. Once the corner has been taken, an attacker can score from anywhere in the striking circle.

Penalty corners – here you can see some of the defenders.

A common way of scoring a goal in hockey is from a **penalty corner**, which used to be called a 'short corner'. It is usually awarded because a defender has fouled in their own circle. It is taken from a point on the goal line 9 m (10 yds) from the nearest goal post. The rules for this corner state that four defenders and the goalkeeper can stand on the goal line. The other players must be behind the centre line. All attackers must be outside the striking circle except for the player putting the ball in, who must have his or her feet astride the line. No attacker can shoot at the goal from a corner until the ball has been stopped outside the circle.

There are two **umpires** in hockey who operate on opposite sides of the pitch. They have complete control of the game and can award penalties, penalty corners and free hits independently of each other. If a player commits a serious foul, or is constantly giving away free hits, the umpires will show them a green card as a warning. For a more serious offence, or dangerous play, a player may be shown a yellow card and sent off the pitch temporarily, or shown a red card and sent off permanently.

Breaking the rules

There are many offences that players can commit in hockey. Most of them are due to the fact that it is a non-contact sport.

Players must not interfere with other players or their sticks. They must not obstruct other players from playing the ball.

If you raise your stick dangerously, or if you hit the ball in a way likely to injure another player, you will be penalized. You cannot stop, pick up, or carry the ball in your hand. You must not charge, kick or trip an opponent, or hit, hook or hold an opponent's stick.

If a player is offside he or she may be penalized and the opposing team will be given a free hit from where the offside occurred. You would be offside if you were in your attacking 22.9 m (25 yd) area, and the ball was played to you by a team mate who was further away from the opponents' goal line, and there were fewer than two opposing players nearer to their goal than you. However, you would only be offside if you gained an advantage from the situation, for example, if you scored a goal.

How the offside rule works.

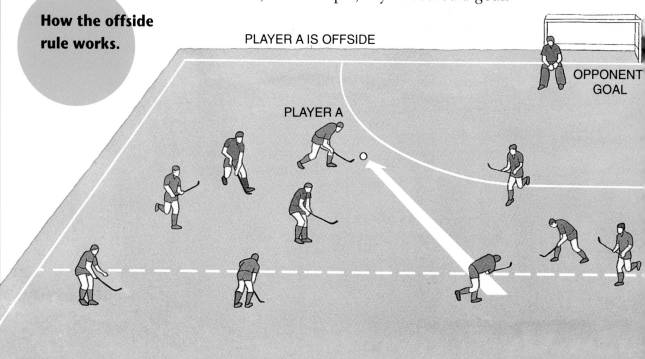

PLAYER A IS OFFSIDE

OPPONENT GOAL

PLAYER A

If any of these fouls are committed by a defender in the circle then a penalty corner is awarded. If the umpires think a foul in the circle is deliberate, or it has prevented a goal, then they can award a **penalty stroke**. This is just like a penalty in football, and is taken from a spot 6.5 m (7 yds) directly in front of the goal. Apart from the penalty-taker and the goalkeeper, all the other players must stay behind the 22.9 m (25 yd) line. Play does not simply carry on after a penalty has been taken. If the goal is scored, then play restarts from the centre with a pass-back by the defenders. If the goal is missed, the defenders hit the ball back into play from a point 14.6 m (16 yds) from where it went out.

When a foul is committed by both teams at the same time, play is restarted by a bully-off. This used to be how a game was started. In a bully two players, one from each side, stand facing each other, with the ball on the ground between them. The two players tap their sticks on the ground and then together three times before the ball can be played. Each player then tries to win the ball.

The bully-off.

Leagues, cups and medals

In most of the world, hockey players do not make fortunes from playing hockey and there are no enormous transfer fees when a player moves from one club to another. Great numbers of people play the game all over the world but huge crowds do not attend matches in the UK. Hockey is known as one of the world's great **participation** sports.

However, every two years there are major international events: the World Cup and, even more important, the Olympic Games.

The first Olympic hockey event was won by Scotland, who beat Germany 4–0 in 1908. The first goal was scored after two minutes by Ian Laing. For the next few Olympic games, teams from the UK won, but from 1928 either India or Pakistan won. Until 1988, one or other of the two countries won a medal at the Olympics. During these years India won gold medals eight times, and Pakistan three times.

Jane Sixsmith playing for Great Britain against Germany at the Barcelona Olympics in 1992.

HOCKEY FACTS

In 1932 India made the highest ever score in an international match when they beat the United States 24–1. In the Olympic final of 1932 they also made the highest ever score when they beat Japan 11–1.

India continuing their Olympic tradition against Germany at Barcelona in 1992.

In 1948, Britain was expected to beat India in the final, but lost 4–0.

Two Indian players, Leslie Claudius and Udham Singh, have won three Olympic gold medals and one silver each. The Indians were so dominant in the Olympics of 1928, 1932 and 1936, they only let in six goals during the whole of these three tournaments. In 1928 they did not let in a single goal over five games, and in the same matches they scored 102 goals of their own.

In the 1988 Olympics the Australian sisters, Lee and Michelle Capes, won gold medals. The Dutch brother and sister, Marc and Carina Benninga, won bronze medals because both of their country's teams came third.

Hockey highlights

Possibly the most destructive shot ever played was in January 1992, during a game in East Grinstead between arch-rivals. They had clashed in cup games twice in 1991, and there was now no love lost between them. The fouls came thick and fast. Many players were treated by their trainers for injuries and knocks. Just after half-time an angry defender took a huge lash at the ball – and caused no less than eight players to leave the game injured!

As the defender hit the ball an opponent put the edge of his stick in the way. This shattered the stick into many pieces. Two bits of wood shot through the top of the opponent's stick and stuck deep into his hand. In his sudden pain he threw what was left of his stick behind him, and hit his own captain in the eye. The captain brought his hands suddenly up to his face and smashed his stick into the jaw of a player to his right, breaking several of his teeth. That player dropped immediately to the floor and another player, running to the scene, fell over him and dislocated his wrist.

Hockey can be painful, especially if you're fouled!

Meanwhile, the ball had shot off the clashing sticks and hit the first defender just below the knee, breaking his leg. Despite this, he carried on swinging around with the momentum of his shot and hit an opponent on his left in the stomach with his stick. The ball rolled away quickly and another player, distracted by the clash, trod on it, fell over and dislocated his elbow.

On seeing this awful scene, a substitute player jumped up too quickly and hit his head on the roof of the dugout, and needed several stitches for the cut he got. Eight players down with one shot! The game was abandoned, and never replayed.

In the build up to the Moscow Olympics of 1980, the Great Britain squad met for a fitness monitoring session. The first test was a five mile run. They had a target time of 28 to 34 minutes. Billy McClean, a Scottish right-winger, puffed in after 43 minutes. When asked by the coaches how he could justify being chosen after such a bad time, he replied, 'I haven't played against anyone yet who can hit the ball five miles!' The training sessions got even harder – and then the team boycotted the games and didn't go.

In an attempt to give his players the right attitude, Wim van Heumen, the Dutch national hockey coach, looked for a saying that would sum up his approach to the game. Eventually he came up with one that applies to any sport. He said,
'To play the game is good.
To win the game is better.
To love the game is best.'

Glossary

bully-off After certain stoppages, the game can be restarted with the ball being placed between two players who tap their sticks together three times before going for the ball.

clearing Moving the ball from a dangerous situation to a safer one.

corner A corner taken by an attacker if a defender has accidentally knocked the ball over the goal-line. Used to be called a long corner.

dribble Keeping the ball under control while running with it.

feet The umpire blows the whistle and indicates 'feet' if a player has kicked the ball or a foot has touched it.

flick The stick is pushed under the ball and the ball is lifted over the defenders' sticks.

getting goal side Getting into a position between an attacker and the goal.

Indian dribble The ball is tapped or dragged repeatedly from left to right by twisting wrist movements as the player runs along.

indoor hockey A form of the game played on a smaller, indoor pitch with some different rules. Often used as practice for the outdoor game.

jab tackle Holding the stick in one hand it is moved to jab the ball away.

kickers The especially hard overshoes worn by goalkeepers.

open-side tackle A tackle made on the defender's right side using the 'open' stick, i.e. toe pointing up.

participation sports A sport in which many people participate or play.

pass The general term for the strokes used to send the ball from one player to another.

pass-back At the beginning of the game the team with the ball must pass it back towards their own goal-line to start.

penalty corner A hit-in taken from close to the goal on the goal-line if an offence has been committed by the defence in their own striking circle.

penalty stroke A push or flick from in front of goal, awarded after an offence by the defenders in their own striking circle.

push pass The ball is propelled along the ground, with the stick kept in contact with the ball as long as possible.

reverse-stick pass The stick is turned over with the toe pointed downwards and a pass is made from left to right with the flat side.

reverse-stick tackle A tackle made by a defender holding the stick in the 'reverse' stick position, i.e. toe pointing down.

slap pass A cross between a hit and a push made with a short backswing.

striking circle The semi-circle, or 'D', at either end of the pitch from which you are allowed to score a goal.

sweeper A defender positioned behind the rest of the team who 'sweeps up' loose balls, and covers any unmarked attackers.

umpires The two officials who control the game and make sure the rules are followed.

Index